for

chad

secret life
of
the ant hill

Meet Louie. Louie is an ant. He lives in a beautiful park under a picnic table.

Ants are the longest living of all insects, living for up to 30 years.

He hides out of sight from the humans. He really likes pies. He loves Apple pie, Cherry pie and Pumpkin pie. In fact, he's never met a pie he didn't like. His favorite though is Cream Cheese Cherry pie.

The humans never eat all their food. It's not good to waste food, but Louie doesn't mind. Today he will have some dessert on the house.

Story Note

Ants are very fond of sweets. They also have a keen sense of smell of honeydew and sugar.

Today's haul is pretty good. Louie is pretty strong. Most ants are. We are glad because those cherries are pretty big. We are also curious how they will fit in the tiny hole. Let's find out.

The ant is one of the worlds' strongest creatures in relation to its size.

How clever our little friend is. A secret elevator in the base of a nearby tree will take him far below the surface. The ants use this to move food that is too big to fit in the usual entrance. Let's follow him down and see where he goes.

Story Note

Some ant hills can be up to 3 feet deep.

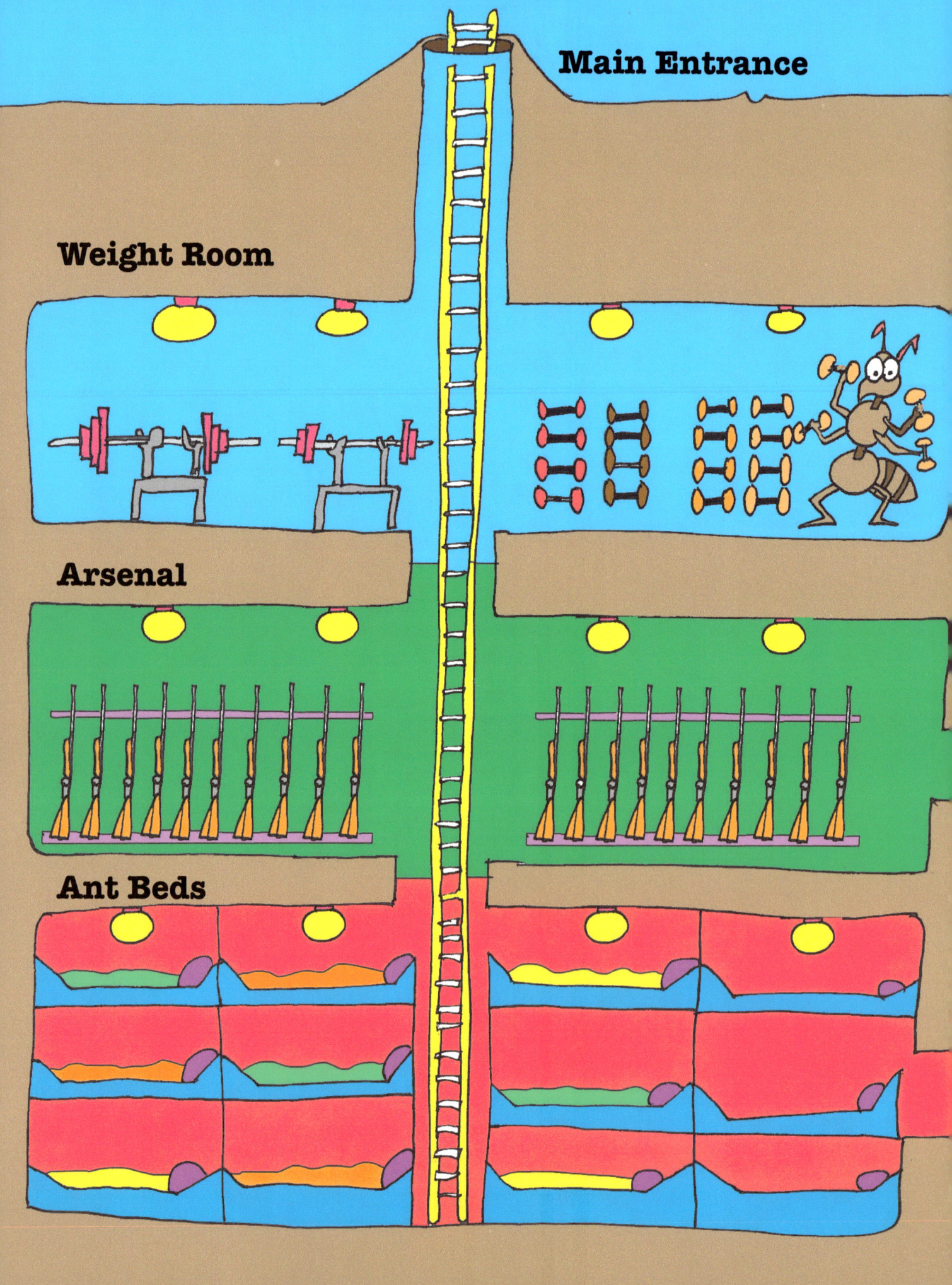

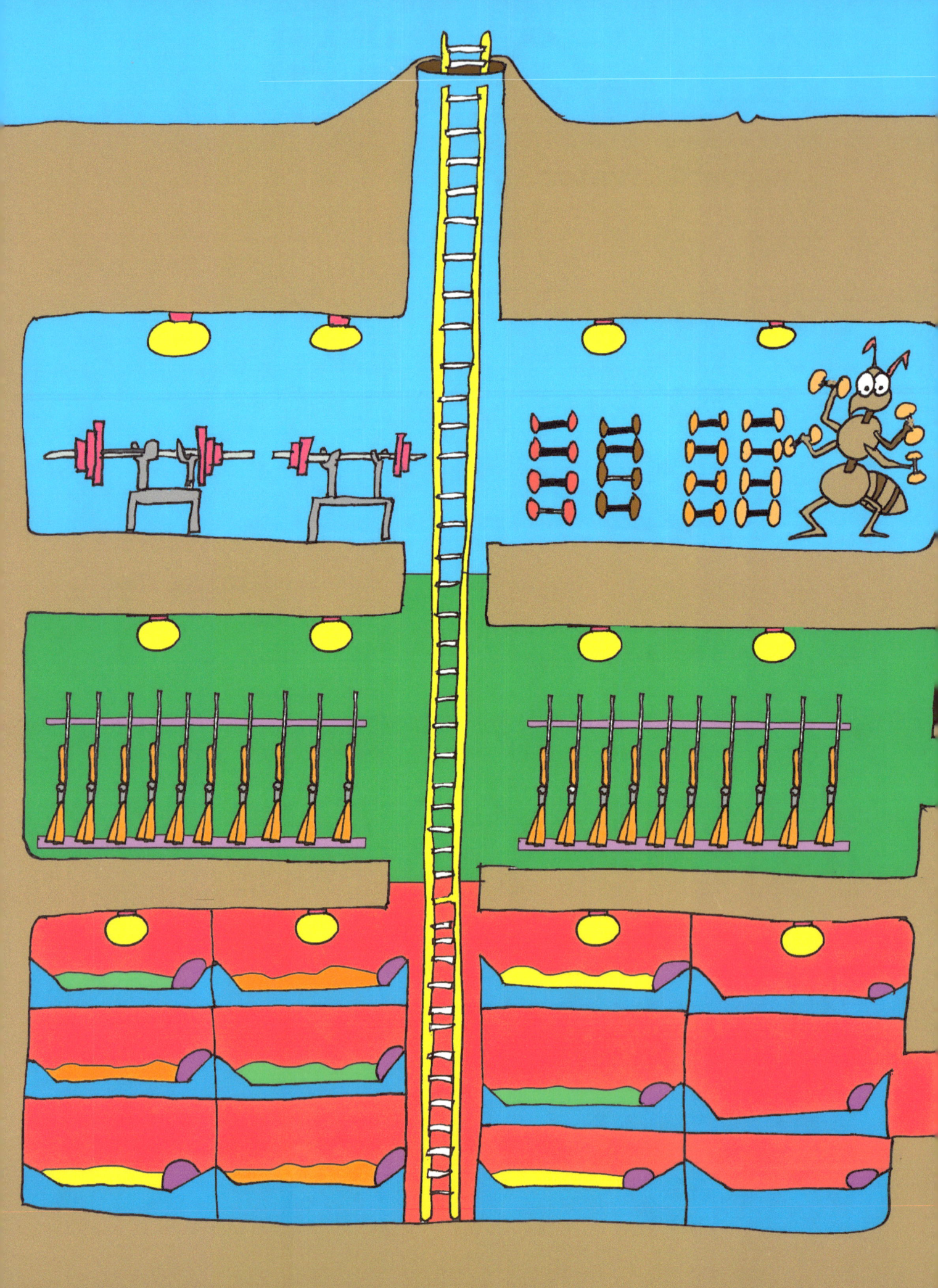

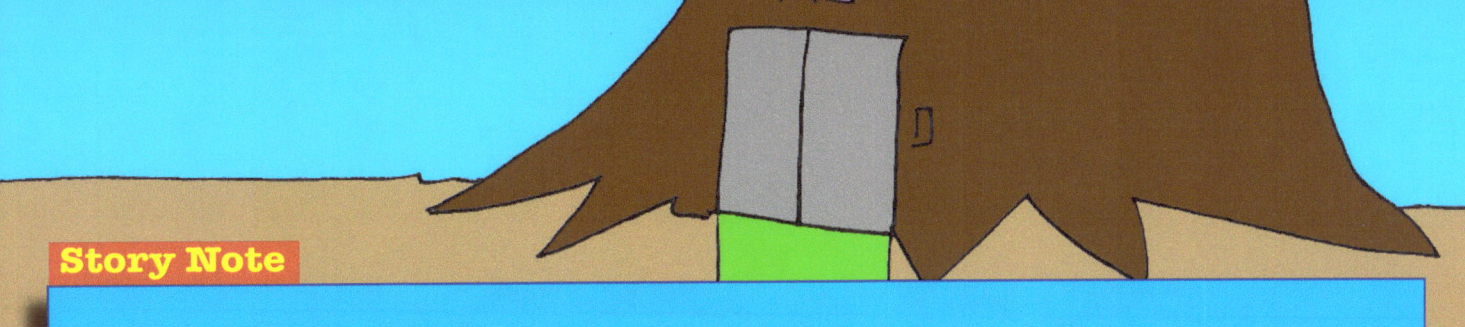

Ants are incredibly capable creatures.
They live in vast, interconnected colonies. They can lift several times their own body weight, and coordinate their activities with incredible precision.

Ants are as old as the dinosaurs.
In 2006, scientists did a massive genetic analysis on ants Their findings suggested that ants first arose about 110—130 million years ago.

With the exception of Antarctica, the Arctic, and a handful of islands, just about every piece of land on Earth harbors at least one native ant species.

The Hawaiian islands, for instance — not one of their more than 50 established ant species is believed to be native to the archipelago.

The total ant population makes our 7 billion look weak.
In their Pulitzer-prize winning book The Ants, researchers Bert Hölldobler and Edward O.Wilson estimate that there are upwards of 10,000,000,000,000,000 individual ants alive on Earth at any given time.

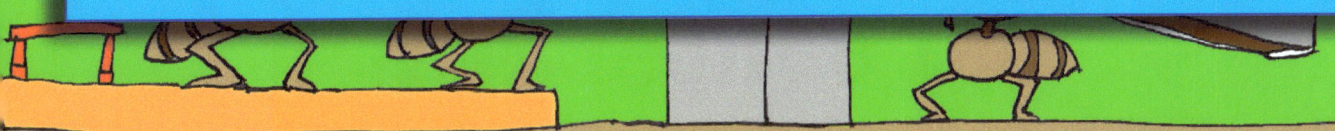

Meet some of Louie's friends.

Winthorpe the Carpenter Ant

Ophelia the
Leaf Cutter Ant

Mortimer the
Fire Ant

Clarence the
Army Ant

Penelope the Harvester Ant

Muffy the
Honey Pot Ant

Constance the
Weaver Ant

Bunny the
Acrobat Ant

Billy Ray the Pharaoh Ant

**Harvey the
Crazy Ant**

Louie and his friends were taking a break to enjoy a cup of coffee when suddenly the picnic area alarm began to sound.

That means there is something special on the picnic table. Everybody was ordered to the surface. "Hurry," said Louie!

When they reached the table top and peered over the edge, they paused. They did not say a word. What they saw was unbelievable.

Never in their wildest dreams could they have imagined what was before them. Then, one by one they began to shake with excitement and couldn't take it anymore. Suddenly they all yelled........

"DONUTS!"

They ate and ate for hours and were all miserably full for days.

THE END.

About the Author.

**Mild mannered advertising executive by day...
mad submarine designer and writer by night.**

Purdy is a self-taught artist. Working in Mixed media, he works from his studio in Micanopy, Florida.

Raised on the shores of historic St. Augustine Florida, Glen Purdy learned early to appreciate the natural beauty of the coast of Florida. With a traditional education in advertising at the University of Florida and art at the University of Florida School of Fine Arts, he began his art career. It has been easy for Glen to find the inspiration for his work. He has been happily married for 35 years and has two wonderful children, and parents who always found loving and exciting ways to invest in his imagination.

His limited edition collectibles are represented in many private collections and displayed throughout the world. Glen has been creating award-winning designs for over 20 years, translating the world around him into handcrafted masterpieces.

More Books By Glen

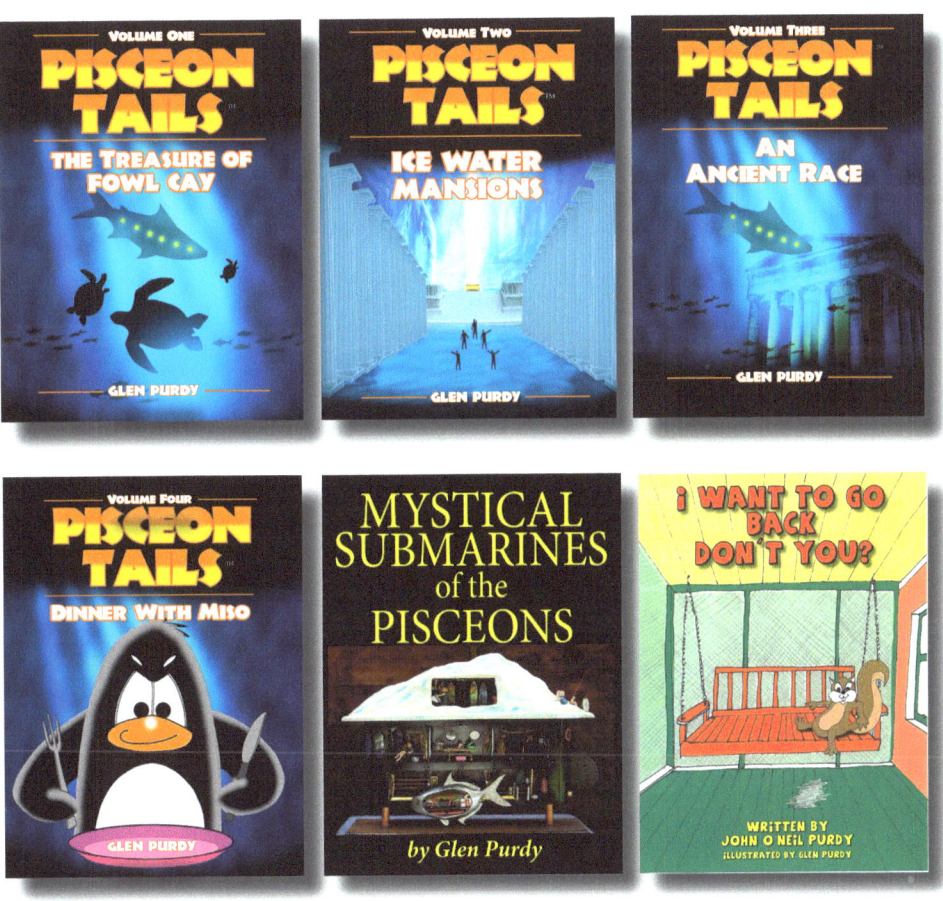

glenpurdy.com

www.ingramcontent.com/pod-product-compliance
Lightning Source LLC
Chambersburg PA
CBHW041534280526
45792CB00004B/1504